BREAKING THE GLASS CEILING

A WOMAN'S GUIDE TO SUCCESS

Monisha Gupta

This book is dedicated to

My parents: For raising me to believe in myself and that the sky is the limit

My sister: For challenging the status quo and always being there for me

My husband: For being my biggest cheerleader and always supporting me

My kids: For being the joys of my heart, and the promise of tomorrow

About the Author

Monisha Gupta is a passionate advocate for women's leadership and gender equality, with a deep interest in understanding and addressing the challenges that women face in achieving equality in all aspects of life.

She is an enthusiastic supporter of gender equality and believes deeply in the importance of creating a world where everyone has equal rights and opportunities, regardless of gender. She is dedicated to exploring these issues and contributing to the conversation surrounding women's empowerment.

Born and raised in India, having spent the last 18 years in the United States, Monisha has always been intrigued by the dynamics of leadership, gender relations, issues of social justice and equality. Through her personal experiences and observations, she has come to recognize the importance of promoting diversity, inclusion, and equal opportunities for all individuals.

In writing this book, Monisha seeks to shed light on the experiences of women leaders, highlight the barriers they face, and celebrate their achievements and contributions to society. She believes that by amplifying the voices of women leaders and advocating for gender equality, we can create a more just and equitable world for future generations.

She hopes to spark meaningful conversations, raise awareness, and inspire action towards a more unbiased and inclusive society. She firmly believes that every individual has a role to play in advancing gender equality, and she is committed to doing her part.

In addition to writing, Monisha is passionate about sports, music and travel. She holds a Masters degree and is eager to embark on this journey of exploration and advocacy. She looks forward to engaging and connecting with readers who share her passion for women's leadership and gender equality.

Contents

CHAPTER 1: THE HISTORY OF THE GLASS CEILING

THE CONCEPT OF THE GLASS CEILING

The concept of the glass ceiling is a pervasive issue that continues to affect women in the workforce. In the book "Breaking the Glass Ceiling: A Woman's Guide to Success," we delve into the root causes of this phenomenon and provide strategies for overcoming it.

The glass ceiling refers to the invisible barrier that prevents women from advancing to higher levels of leadership and success in their careers. Despite the progress that has been made in terms of gender equality, many women still find themselves hitting this barrier as they strive to reach the top of their professions.

One of the key factors contributing to the glass ceiling is the lack of representation of women in leadership positions. When women

1

are not seen in top roles within organizations, it can be difficult for other women to envision themselves in those positions. This lack of representation can create a self-perpetuating cycle that hinders women's advancement.

Additionally, unconscious bias and gender stereotypes can also play a role in reinforcing the glass ceiling. These biases can lead to women being overlooked for promotions or opportunities for advancement, simply because of their gender. It is important for both men and women to be aware of these biases and work towards creating a more inclusive and equitable work environment.

In "Breaking the Glass Ceiling," we provide practical advice and actionable steps for women to break through the barriers that may be holding them back. By empowering women to advocate for themselves, challenge societal norms, and support one another, we can work towards a future where the glass ceiling is shattered once and for all. Let's work together to create a world where all women have the opportunity to reach their full potential and achieve their dreams.

THE ORIGINS OF THE GLASS CEILING

The glass ceiling is a metaphorical barrier that prevents women and minorities from advancing in their careers and reaching top leadership positions. The origins of the glass ceiling can be traced back to centuries of systemic discrimination and gender bias in the workplace.

Throughout history, women have been relegated to domestic roles and excluded from positions of power and influence. Even as women began entering the workforce in larger numbers in the 20th century, they faced myriad obstacles to advancement. From unequal pay to limited opportunities for promotion, women were often held back by societal expectations and institutionalized sexism.

The term "glass ceiling" was first popularized in the 1980s as women began to push for greater representation in corporate America. Despite their qualifications and achievements, women found themselves hitting an invisible barrier that prevented them from rising to the top. This glass ceiling was rooted in deep-seated beliefs about gender roles and the perceived limitations of women in leadership roles.

As we continue to break down barriers and challenge stereotypes, it is important to understand the historical context that has shaped the glass ceiling. By acknowledging the origins of this phenomenon, we can work towards dismantling it and creating a more inclusive and equitable society for all.

For women, men, parents, and teenagers interested in feminism and gender equality, understanding the historical background of the glass ceiling is essential to becoming advocates for change. By educating ourselves and others about the historical context of gender inequality, we can work together to break the glass ceiling once and for all.

THE IMPACT OF THE GLASS CEILING ON WOMEN

The glass ceiling is an invisible barrier that prevents women from reaching the highest levels of leadership in their careers. This barrier is often created by societal norms, gender biases, and discrimination, making it difficult for women to break through and achieve their full potential. In our society, women are often held back from pursuing leadership roles due to stereotypes and expectations that limit their opportunities for growth and advancement.

The impact of the glass ceiling on women is profound and far-reaching. It not only affects individual women's careers but also has broader implications for society as a whole. When women are unable to access leadership positions, their perspectives and voices are missing from decision-making processes, leading to a lack of diversity and inclusivity in leadership roles. This can result in policies and practices that do not adequately address the needs and concerns of women and other marginalized groups.

For women, the glass ceiling can lead to feelings of frustration, self-doubt, and imposter syndrome. It can also have negative effects on their mental health and overall well-being. Women may feel undervalued, overlooked, and unappreciated in the workplace, leading to decreased job satisfaction and motivation. This can create a cycle of self-perpetuating inequality that is difficult to break free from.

As parents and educators, it is important to educate young girls about the existence of the glass ceiling and empower them to challenge and overcome it. By instilling confidence, resilience, and a strong sense of self-worth in young girls, we can help them navigate the challenges of the workplace and strive for leadership positions in their chosen fields. By breaking down barriers and advocating for gender equality, we can create a more inclusive and equitable society for all.

PROGRESS IN BREAKING THE GLASS CEILING

The journey towards gender equality and breaking the glass ceiling has been a long and challenging one, but there have been significant strides made in recent years. Women are now rising to leadership positions in various fields, shattering the invisible barriers that once held them back. This progress is not only empowering for women but also inspiring for the younger generations who are witnessing these changes unfold.

CHAPTER 1: THE HISTORY OF THE GLASS CEILING

One of the key factors contributing to this progress is the push for diversity and inclusion in the workplace. Companies are now recognizing the value of having women in leadership positions and are actively working towards creating more opportunities for them to succeed. This shift in mindset is slowly but surely breaking down the barriers that have long prevented women from reaching the top.

Another factor that has fueled progress in breaking the glass ceiling is the rise of feminism and the continued fight for gender equality. Women are no longer willing to accept the status quo and are demanding equal treatment and opportunities in all aspects of their lives. This collective push for change has been instrumental in breaking down stereotypes and challenging outdated beliefs about women's capabilities.

For men, parents and teenagers, these developments serve as a reminder that anything is possible with hard work, determination, and perseverance. The stories of women who have broken through the glass ceiling serve as inspiration for the next generation of leaders, showing them that they too can achieve their dreams no matter the obstacles they face.

As we continue to make progress in breaking the glass ceiling, it is important to celebrate the achievements of women in leadership roles and to continue pushing for change. By working together, we can create a more inclusive and equal society where women have the same opportunities to succeed as their male counterparts.

Through education, advocacy, and mentorship, we can work towards breaking the glass ceiling and creating a more level playing field for women in the workplace. By supporting and uplifting women in their professional journeys, we can create a more diverse, inclusive, and successful workforce for future generations. Together, we can shatter the glass ceiling once and for all.

CHAPTER 2: OVERCOMING STEREOTYPES AND BIAS

CHALLENGING GENDER STEREOTYPES

In today's society, gender stereotypes continue to permeate various aspects of our lives, dictating how individuals should behave based on their gender. However, challenging these stereotypes is crucial in order to break down barriers and create a more inclusive and equal world. In this subchapter, we will explore the importance of challenging gender stereotypes and the impact it can have on individuals and society as a whole.

For women, challenging gender stereotypes means refusing to be confined by societal expectations and limitations placed upon them. It means breaking free from the notion that certain roles and professions are only meant for men, and demonstrating that women are just as capable and deserving of leadership positions and success.

By challenging these stereotypes, women can empower themselves and inspire others to do the same.

For parents, challenging gender stereotypes means raising children in a way that promotes equality and respect for all genders. It means encouraging children to pursue their passions and interests without being constrained by outdated notions of what is considered "appropriate" for their gender. By teaching children to challenge gender stereotypes, parents can help shape a future generation that is more open-minded and accepting of diversity.

For teenagers, challenging gender stereotypes means being true to themselves and not conforming to societal expectations of how they should look or act based on their gender. It means embracing their uniqueness and standing up against discrimination and inequality. By challenging gender stereotypes, teenagers can pave the way for a more inclusive and accepting society where everyone is free to be themselves without fear of judgment or prejudice.

In conclusion, challenging gender stereotypes is an essential step towards achieving gender equality and creating a more just and equitable world for all. It requires courage, determination, and a willingness to challenge the status quo. But by breaking free from the confines of gender stereotypes, we can pave the way for a brighter and more inclusive future for generations to come.

DEALING WITH WORKPLACE BIAS

In the journey to break the glass ceiling and rise to leadership positions, women often face workplace bias that can hinder their progress. It is important to recognize and address these biases in order to create a more inclusive and equitable work environment. In this subchapter, we will explore some strategies for dealing with workplace bias and overcoming obstacles on the path to leadership.

CHAPTER 2: OVERCOMING STEREOTYPES AND BIAS

First and foremost, it is crucial to be aware of the biases that exist in the workplace. Whether it is subtle microaggressions or overt discrimination, acknowledging the presence of bias is the first step towards addressing it. Educate yourself on common biases that women face, such as the gender pay gap, lack of representation in leadership roles, and stereotypes about women's abilities.

One way to combat workplace bias is to build a strong support system. Surround yourself with mentors, allies, and peers who can offer guidance, advice, and encouragement. Lean on these individuals for support when faced with bias or discrimination in the workplace.

Additionally, it is important to advocate for yourself and others. Speak up when you witness bias or discrimination, whether it is directed towards you or someone else. Use your voice to challenge stereotypes, promote diversity and inclusion, and push for equal opportunities for all.

Remember that change takes time and perseverance. Breaking the glass ceiling is not easy, but with determination, resilience, and a supportive community, women can overcome workplace bias and rise to leadership positions. By standing up against bias and advocating for equality, we can create a more inclusive and empowering work environment for all.

STRATEGIES FOR OVERCOMING STEREOTYPES

Stereotypes have long been a barrier for women seeking to advance in leadership roles. In order to break through these barriers, it is important for women to employ strategies for overcoming stereotypes and proving their worth in male-dominated environments. This subchapter will explore some effective strategies for challenging and dismantling stereotypes in the workplace.

CHAPTER 2: OVERCOMING STEREOTYPES AND BIAS

One key strategy for overcoming stereotypes is to consistently demonstrate competence and expertise in your field. By excelling in your work and consistently producing high-quality results, you can challenge the notion that women are less capable than men. Additionally, seeking out opportunities to showcase your skills and expertise can help to break down stereotypes and prove your value as a leader.

Another important strategy is to actively challenge stereotypes when they arise. This can involve speaking up when you witness discriminatory behavior or language, or advocating for yourself and other women in the workplace. By addressing stereotypes head-on, you can help to create a more inclusive and equitable work environment for all.

It is also important for women to seek out mentors and allies who can support them in their efforts to overcome stereotypes. Having a strong support network can provide encouragement, guidance, and advocacy in challenging situations. Additionally, building relationships with other women in leadership roles can help to create a sense of solidarity and empowerment.

Overall, the key to overcoming stereotypes is to be confident in your abilities, advocate for yourself and others, and seek out support from mentors and allies. This will require courage, resilience, and a willingness to challenge the status quo. By employing these strategies, women can break through the glass ceiling and achieve success in leadership roles.

EMPOWERING YOURSELF TO BREAK THROUGH STEREOTYPES

In a society where gender stereotypes still prevail, it is crucial for women to empower themselves and take control of their narratives. For all interested in feminism and gender equality, this subchapter serves as a call to action to break free from the confines of limiting beliefs and societal expectations.

CHAPTER 2: OVERCOMING STEREOTYPES AND BIAS

It is a reminder that each individual has the power to define their own worth and capabilities, regardless of their gender. To empower yourself to break through stereotypes, start by recognizing and acknowledging the stereotypes that may be holding you back. Whether it's the belief that women are not as capable as men in leadership roles or the idea that men should not show vulnerability, identifying these stereotypes is the first step towards challenging them.

Next, cultivate a strong sense of self-confidence and self-worth. Surround yourself with supportive and empowering individuals who believe in your abilities and encourage you to reach your full potential. Take risks, step out of your comfort zone, and challenge yourself to defy expectations and prove the naysayers wrong.

Lastly, advocate for gender equality and challenge stereotypes in your everyday interactions. Speak up against discriminatory practices, support initiatives that promote diversity and inclusion, and be a role model for future generations by showing that success knows no gender.

By empowering yourself to break through stereotypes, you not only pave the way for your own success but also contribute to a more inclusive and equitable society for all. Remember, you have the power to shatter glass ceilings and redefine what it means to be a successful and empowered individual, regardless of your gender.

CHAPTER 3: LEADING WITH CONFIDENCE AND AUTHENTICITY

IMPORTANCE OF CONFIDENCE IN THE WORKPLACE

Confidence is a crucial factor in achieving success in the workplace, regardless of gender. In a male-dominated society, women often face challenges and barriers that can hinder their progress. Building confidence is essential for women to break through the glass ceiling and reach their full potential.

Confidence allows individuals to take risks, speak up, and assert themselves in various situations. In the workplace, confident individuals are more likely to be noticed, respected, and given opportunities for growth and advancement. Women who exude confidence are perceived as competent and capable, which can lead to increased job satisfaction and overall success.

For men, confidence is also key to success in the workplace. However, studies have shown that men are more likely to exhibit confidence in their abilities even when they may not have the necessary skills or experience. Women, on the other hand, often doubt themselves and underestimate their capabilities. By building confidence, women can level the playing field and compete on an equal footing with their male counterparts.

Parents play a crucial role in instilling confidence in their children from a young age. By encouraging their daughters to be assertive, take risks, and believe in themselves, parents can help prepare them for future success in the workplace. Similarly, teenagers can benefit from building confidence early on, as it can set them up for a successful career later in life.

In the fight for gender equality, confidence is a powerful tool that can help women overcome societal stereotypes and biases. By believing in themselves and their abilities, women can shatter the glass ceiling and pave the way for future generations of strong, confident female leaders.

BUILDING CONFIDENCE AS A FEMALE LEADER

In a world where women often face barriers to success, building self-confidence is essential for breaking through the glass ceiling. However, for female leaders, building and maintaining confidence can be particularly challenging in a society that often undermines their abilities and potential. Confidence is not something that comes naturally to everyone, but it can be developed through intentional strategies and practices. In this subchapter, we will explore strategies and tips for women to boost their confidence and thrive as leaders in the face of adversity.

1. One of the first steps in building confidence as a female leader is to recognize and challenge internalized stereotypes and biases that may be holding you back. Society often imposes unrealistic

expectations and standards on women, leading them to doubt their own capabilities. By acknowledging and confronting these negative beliefs, you can begin to reframe your mindset and approach leadership with a newfound sense of self-assurance.

2. Learn to set realistic goals for yourself. One of the first steps to building self-confidence is setting achievable goals for yourself. Start small and gradually work your way up to bigger challenges. Celebrate your successes, no matter how small, and use them as motivation to keep pushing yourself.

3. Another important aspect of building confidence is surrounding yourself with a supportive network of mentors, colleagues, and friends who believe in your potential. Seek out role models who have successfully navigated the challenges of leadership as women, and draw inspiration from their journeys. Additionally, don't be afraid to seek feedback and constructive criticism from others, as this can help you identify areas for growth and improvement.

4. Practicing self-care and prioritizing your well-being is also crucial for building confidence as a female leader. Make time for activities that nourish your mind, body, and spirit, whether it's exercise, meditation, or spending time with loved ones. Remember that you are worthy of self-love and acceptance, and that taking care of yourself is not a sign of weakness, but of strength.

5. By cultivating a strong sense of self-belief, seeking support from others, and prioritizing your well-being, you can build the confidence you need to succeed as a female leader. Embrace your unique strengths and abilities, and let your light shine brightly in the world of leadership. Remember, you are capable of breaking through the glass ceiling and inspiring others to do the same.

6. Lastly, learn to embrace failure as a learning opportunity. Failure is a natural part of the journey to success. Instead of letting setbacks crush your confidence, use them as learning

opportunities. Reflect on what went wrong, make adjustments, and keep moving forward with newfound knowledge and resilience.

By implementing these strategies for building self-confidence, you can empower yourself to break through the glass ceiling and achieve your goals. Remember that confidence is a skill that can be developed over time with practice and perseverance. Believe in yourself and your abilities, and the sky's the limit.

ASSERTIVENESS TECHNIQUES

Assertiveness techniques for women are crucial in breaking through the barriers that prevent them from achieving their full potential. In a society where women are often expected to be passive and accommodating, it is essential for women to learn how to assert themselves confidently and effectively.

One key assertiveness technique for women is learning to communicate clearly and directly. Women should not shy away from expressing their thoughts, opinions, and needs in a straightforward manner. By speaking up and making their voices heard, women can ensure that their perspectives are valued and respected in both personal and professional settings.

Another important assertiveness technique for women is setting boundaries. Women should not be afraid to say no to requests or demands that do not align with their values or priorities. By establishing boundaries and sticking to them, women can protect their time, energy, and well-being.

Additionally, women can benefit from practicing assertive body language. Maintaining eye contact, standing tall, and using confident gestures can help women convey strength and authority in their interactions with others. By exuding self-assurance through their body language, women can command respect and assert their presence in any situation.

Overall, assertiveness techniques for women are essential tools for navigating the challenges of a male-dominated world and achieving success on their own terms. By mastering the art of assertiveness, women can break through the glass ceiling and rise to new heights in their personal and professional lives.

EMBRACING AUTHENTICITY IN LEADERSHIP

In today's world, the concept of leadership has evolved beyond traditional definitions. As women continue to break through the glass ceiling and shatter stereotypes, the importance of embracing authenticity in leadership has become more apparent than ever. In this subchapter, we delve into the power of authenticity and how it can transform not only your leadership style but also your personal growth and fulfillment.

Authenticity in leadership is about being true to yourself, your values, and your beliefs. It is about showing up as your genuine self, without masks or pretenses. When you embrace authenticity, you build trust and credibility with those around you, inspiring others to follow your lead.

For women in leadership roles, embracing authenticity is especially crucial. In a world where gender biases and expectations still persist, staying true to who you are can be a powerful tool in breaking down barriers and challenging the status quo. By leading with authenticity, women can pave the way for more inclusive and diverse leadership styles, creating a more equitable and empowering work environment for all.

As parents, instilling the value of authenticity in our children is essential. By modeling authenticity in our own lives and encouraging our children to embrace their true selves, we empower them to become confident and resilient leaders in their own right.

For teenagers navigating their way through a world filled with societal pressures and expectations, embracing authenticity can be a game-changer. By staying true to who they are and following their passions, teenagers can build a strong sense of self-worth and confidence that will serve them well in their future leadership endeavors.

In conclusion, embracing authenticity in leadership is not just a choice — it is a necessity. By staying true to ourselves and leading with authenticity, we can inspire others, break down barriers, and create a more inclusive and empowering world for all.

FINDING YOUR LEADERSHIP STYLE

One of the most important aspects of becoming a successful leader is discovering and embracing your own unique leadership style. In the world of business, politics, and beyond, there are countless different leadership styles that can be effective.

As women, it is important to find a leadership style that not only feels authentic to us but also allows us to thrive in our respective fields.

There are several different leadership styles that women can adopt, including transformational, democratic, autocratic, and servant leadership. Each style has its own strengths and weaknesses, and it is important to experiment with different styles to see which one resonates most with you. For some women, a transformational leadership style — one that focuses on inspiring and motivating others — may be the most effective. For others, a democratic leadership style — one that encourages collaboration and input from team members — may be more suitable.

It is also important to consider your personal strengths and weaknesses when determining your leadership style. Are you a natural communicator? Do you excel at building strong relationships with others? These qualities can help guide you towards a leadership style that plays to your strengths.

As parents, it is important to encourage our daughters to explore different leadership styles and find the one that works best for them. By empowering them to embrace their unique leadership qualities, we are helping to shape the future of female leadership.

For teenagers interested in pursuing a career in leadership, it is important to remember that there is no one-size-fits-all approach to leadership. Take the time to explore different styles, seek out mentors who can provide guidance, and always stay true to yourself.

In the world of feminism, finding your leadership style is not only important for your personal success but also for the advancement of women as a whole. By embracing your unique leadership qualities, you are helping to break down barriers and inspire others to do the same.

CHAPTER 4: NAVIGATING WORK-LIFE BALANCE

THE MYTH OF WORK-LIFE BALANCE

The myth of work–life balance is a concept that has long plagued women in their quest for success and fulfillment. The idea that one can perfectly balance their career and personal life is simply unrealistic and unattainable. In reality, achieving success in one area often requires sacrifices in another, leading to feelings of guilt and inadequacy.

For women, the pressure to excel in both their professional and personal lives can be overwhelming. Society often places unrealistic expectations on women to be perfect employees, mothers, wives, and caregivers all at once. This can lead to burnout, stress, and feelings of failure when they inevitably fall short of these impossible standards.

CHAPTER 4: NAVIGATING WORK-LIFE BALANCE

It is important for women to recognize that it is okay to prioritize certain aspects of their lives at different times. Sometimes, the focus may be on advancing their career, while at other times, it may be on their family or personal well-being. Finding a balance that works for each individual is key, rather than striving for an unattainable ideal.

For men, parents, and teenagers, the myth of work-life balance also applies. It is important for everyone to understand that it is okay to prioritize certain aspects of their lives at different times. By letting go of the idea of perfection and embracing the concept of work-life integration, individuals can find a sense of fulfillment and success without the constant pressure to achieve the impossible.

In the fight for gender equality and feminism, challenging the myth of work-life balance is crucial. By acknowledging and dismantling this unrealistic expectation, women can pave the way for a more equitable and supportive work environment for all individuals. Breaking the glass ceiling starts with rejecting the myth of work-life balance and embracing a more realistic and sustainable approach to success.

BALANCING CAREER AND FAMILY

In today's fast-paced world, balancing a successful career with family responsibilities can often feel like an impossible task. However, in reality, many women have managed to break the glass ceiling and achieve leadership positions while also maintaining a fulfilling family life. In this subchapter, we will explore the inspiring stories of women who have successfully navigated the challenges of balancing career and family.

For women, especially mothers, juggling work and family responsibilities can be a daunting task. However, it is important to remember that it is possible to have a successful career and a happy family life. Many successful women leaders have shared their stories of how they have managed to prioritize both their careers and their families.

CHAPTER 4: NAVIGATING WORK-LIFE BALANCE

One key aspect of balancing career and family is effective time management. Creating a schedule that allows for both work and family time is essential. It may require making sacrifices and setting boundaries, but with determination and perseverance, it is possible to find a balance that works for you.

Another important strategy is prioritizing tasks. Make a list of your daily, weekly, and monthly tasks and prioritize them based on their importance. This will help you focus on the most critical tasks first and avoid feeling overwhelmed by trying to do everything at once.

Additionally, it's essential to practice self-care. Taking care of your physical and mental well-being is crucial for managing work and personal life effectively. Make time for activities that bring you joy and relaxation, such as exercise, meditation, or spending time with loved ones.

Another important factor in balancing career and family is having a strong support system. Whether it is a supportive partner, family members, or reliable childcare, having people you can rely on to help you manage both your career and family responsibilities is crucial.

For parents, it's important to involve your family in your work-life balance strategy. Communicate with your partner and children about your responsibilities and expectations, and delegate tasks when necessary. By working together as a team, you can ensure that everyone's needs are met while still achieving success in your career.

Ultimately, achieving a balance between career and family is a personal journey that will look different for everyone. By learning from the experiences of successful women leaders who have managed to break the glass ceiling while also prioritizing their families, we can gain valuable insights and inspiration to help us navigate our own paths to success.

SETTING BOUNDARIES FOR SELF-CARE

Setting boundaries for self-care is an essential aspect of maintaining a healthy work-life balance, especially for women in leadership roles. In the fast-paced world we live in, it can be easy to neglect our own well-being in favor of meeting the demands of our professional and personal lives. However, prioritizing self-care is not only necessary for our physical and mental health but also crucial for our success as leaders.

As women, we are often expected to juggle multiple responsibilities and put the needs of others before our own. While it's admirable to be caring and nurturing, it's essential to remember that we cannot pour from an empty cup. This can lead to burnout and feelings of being overwhelmed. By setting boundaries for self-care, we can ensure that we are taking the time to recharge and nurture ourselves, allowing us to show up as our best selves in both our personal and professional lives.

For men, it's important to recognize that self-care is not a sign of weakness but rather a strength. By taking care of yourself, you are better equipped to handle the challenges that life throws your way. Self-care is not selfish; it's necessary for maintaining your physical, mental, and emotional health.

For parents and teenagers, setting boundaries for self-care is equally important. It is essential to teach our children the importance of taking care of themselves and prioritizing their well-being. By modeling healthy boundaries and self-care practices, we can instill these values in the next generation of leaders.

In the realm of feminism, setting boundaries for self-care is a radical act of self-love and empowerment. It is a way of reclaiming our time and energy, and asserting our worth in a society that often devalues women's well-being. By setting boundaries, we are asserting our right to prioritize ourselves and our needs, and challenging the expectation that women should always put others first.

In conclusion, self-care is not a luxury but a necessity for overall well-being. By making yourself a priority, you are setting yourself up for success in all areas of your life. Remember to take time for yourself, practice self-love, and prioritize your well-being. It is a way of honoring ourselves and our worth, and ensuring that we are able to show up as our best selves in all areas of our lives. By prioritizing self-care, we are not only taking care of ourselves but also setting an example for others to do the same.

CREATING SUPPORTIVE NETWORKS

In the journey towards breaking the glass ceiling and achieving success in leadership roles, one of the most crucial elements is creating supportive networks. These networks can provide women with the necessary encouragement, guidance, and resources to navigate the challenges and obstacles that often come with leadership positions.

For women, having a supportive network can make all the difference in their careers. Whether it's a group of like-minded individuals who share similar goals and aspirations, or mentors who can offer valuable advice and insight, having a strong support system can help women build confidence, overcome imposter syndrome, and push through any barriers they may face.

Parents play a crucial role in helping their daughters build supportive networks from a young age. By encouraging them to join clubs, organizations, and programs that align with their interests and passions, parents can help their daughters connect with like-minded individuals who can serve as mentors and role models. Additionally, parents can also model the importance of networking and building relationships by introducing their daughters to their own professional contacts and encouraging them to attend networking events.

CHAPTER 4: NAVIGATING WORK-LIFE BALANCE

For teenagers, creating supportive networks can be especially beneficial as they navigate the challenges of adolescence and begin to explore their career aspirations. By connecting with peers who share similar interests and goals, teenagers can build a strong foundation of support that will serve them well as they move into adulthood and pursue leadership roles.

In the realm of feminism, creating supportive networks is essential for advancing the cause of gender equality and empowering women to reach their full potential. By coming together to support and uplift one another, women can break down barriers, challenge stereotypes, and create a more inclusive and equitable society for all. Through the power of supportive networks, women can truly shatter the glass ceiling and inspire future generations to do the same.

CHAPTER 5: NAVIGATING WORKPLACE CHALLENGES

DEALING WITH SEXISM AND DISCRIMINATION

Dealing with sexism and discrimination is an unfortunate reality that many women face in their personal and professional lives. It is important for women to understand how to navigate these challenges in order to achieve success and break through the glass ceiling that often holds them back.

First and foremost, it is crucial for women to recognize when they are facing sexism and discrimination. This may come in the form of subtle comments or actions that undermine their abilities or potential. By being aware of these instances, women can better address them and take steps to combat them.

One way to deal with sexism and discrimination is to speak up and advocate for yourself. It can be intimidating to confront those who are being discriminatory, but it is important to stand up for yourself and assert your worth. By speaking out against sexism and discrimination, you can help create a more inclusive and equal environment for yourself and others.

Another important aspect of dealing with sexism and discrimination is to seek support from others. Whether it be from friends, family, mentors, or support groups, having a strong support system can help women navigate these challenges and stay resilient in the face of adversity.

For parents and teenagers, it is crucial to teach young girls about the importance of standing up against sexism and discrimination. By instilling confidence and resilience in young girls, parents can help prepare them for the challenges they may face in the future.

In conclusion, dealing with sexism and discrimination is a difficult but necessary part of breaking the glass ceiling. By being aware of these challenges, speaking up, seeking support, and empowering the next generation, women can overcome these obstacles and achieve success in their personal and professional lives.

HANDLING MICRO-AGGRESSIONS IN THE WORKPLACE

In the chapter "Handling Microaggressions in the Workplace" of the book "Breaking the Glass Ceiling: A Woman's Guide to Success," we delve into the pervasive issue of microaggressions that women face in professional settings. Microaggressions are subtle, often unintentional comments or actions that communicate negative stereotypes or biases towards marginalized groups. While they may seem small on the surface, these micro-aggressions can have a significant impact on an individual's well-being and career progression.

For women, navigating micro-aggressions in the workplace can be especially challenging. Whether it's being interrupted in meetings, receiving sexist comments, or being passed over for opportunities, these experiences can chip away at our confidence and sense of belonging. It's important for both women and men to recognize and address these harmful behaviors to create a more inclusive and equitable work environment.

Parents and teenagers can also benefit from understanding how to handle micro-aggressions in the workplace. By educating young people about the impact of these behaviors and empowering them to speak up when they witness or experience them, we can help create a future generation of leaders who prioritize respect and equality.

In the realm of feminism and gender equality, addressing microaggressions is crucial for dismantling the systemic barriers that hold women back. By sharing strategies for confronting and addressing microaggressions, we can work towards creating a more supportive and empowering workplace for all individuals.

Ultimately, by shining a light on the issue of microaggressions and providing practical guidance for handling them, we can empower women to advocate for themselves, challenge harmful stereotypes, and pave the way for a more inclusive and equitable workplace.

OVERCOMING OBSTACLES AND SETBACKS

In the journey towards success, obstacles and setbacks are inevitable. They can come in many forms – discrimination, lack of support, self-doubt, or even just plain bad luck. However, it is how we choose to respond to these challenges that truly defines our path to success.

For women, especially those navigating male-dominated industries, obstacles and setbacks can feel particularly daunting.

The key is to remember that you are not alone in facing these challenges. Many successful women have faced similar obstacles and have come out stronger on the other side. Seek out mentors and allies who can offer support and guidance during difficult times. Surround yourself with a strong support system that believes in your capabilities and encourages you to keep pushing forward.

For men, it is important to recognize the barriers that women face in the workplace and to be allies in breaking down those barriers. Support and advocate for your female colleagues, listen to their experiences, and work towards creating a more inclusive and supportive environment for everyone.

For parents, teaching your children, especially your daughters, about resilience and perseverance in the face of obstacles is crucial. Encourage them to embrace challenges, learn from failures, and never give up on their dreams. Show them through your own actions that setbacks are just temporary roadblocks on the path to success.

For teenagers, it is important to remember that setbacks are a natural part of life. Embrace challenges as opportunities for growth and learning. Surround yourself with positive influences who believe in your potential and encourage you to keep striving for your goals.

Remember, overcoming obstacles and setbacks is not easy, but it is possible. With determination, resilience, and support, you can break through the glass ceiling and achieve your dreams.

CHAPTER 6: NEGOTIATING AND ADVOCATING FOR YOURSELF

IMPORTANCE OF NEGOTIATION SKILLS FOR WOMEN

Negotiation skills are crucial for success in both personal and professional life, and this holds especially true for women. In a society that has historically undervalued women's contributions and marginalized their voices, having strong negotiation skills can help women assert themselves and demand the recognition and opportunities they deserve.

For women, being able to negotiate effectively can mean the difference between being paid fairly for their work or being underpaid, between being promoted to leadership positions or being passed over for less qualified male colleagues. By honing their negotiation skills, women can advocate for themselves in salary negotiations, job interviews, and performance evaluations, ensuring that they are valued and rewarded for their hard work and contributions.

Moreover, negotiation skills can also help women navigate challenging situations in their personal lives, such as setting boundaries in relationships, advocating for their needs, and standing up for themselves in the face of discrimination or harassment. By learning how to negotiate confidently and assertively, women can empower themselves to take control of their own destinies and break free from the constraints of societal expectations and gender stereotypes.

It is important for women of all ages to develop strong negotiation skills, starting from a young age. Parents and educators can play a crucial role in teaching girls the importance of assertiveness, confidence, and effective communication, helping them build the skills they need to succeed in a world that is not always fair or equal.

By empowering women with strong negotiation skills, we can help level the playing field and create a more inclusive and equitable society where everyone has the opportunity to thrive. It is time to break the glass ceiling and pave the way for a future where women can reach their full potential and achieve their dreams.

TIPS FOR SUCCESSFUL NEGOTIATION

Negotiation is a crucial skill that can help individuals, especially women, advance in their careers and achieve their goals. Here are some tips for successful negotiation that can help women break the glass ceiling and reach new heights in their professional lives.

1. Do Your Research: Before entering into a negotiation, it is important to research the market value of your skills and experience. Knowing your worth will give you the confidence to ask for what you deserve.

2. Set Clear Goals: Define your objectives and what you hope to achieve through the negotiation. Having a clear understanding of your goals will help you stay focused and avoid getting sidetracked during the negotiation process.

3. Practice Assertiveness: It is important to be assertive and confident during negotiations. Speak up for yourself and clearly communicate your needs and expectations.

4. Listen Carefully: Effective negotiation is a two-way street. Listen to the other party's perspective and try to understand their needs and concerns. This will help you find common ground and reach a mutually beneficial agreement.

5. Be Willing to Compromise: Negotiation often involves give and take. Be prepared to make concessions, but also know your limits and when to walk away if the terms are not in your favor.

6. Seek Support: It can be helpful to seek advice from mentors, colleagues, or professional coaches who have experience in negotiation. They can provide valuable insights and guidance to help you navigate the negotiation process successfully.

By following these tips for successful negotiation, women can become more confident and effective in advocating for themselves in the workplace. Breaking the glass ceiling and achieving gender equality requires women to be strong negotiators and stand up for their worth. With practice and determination, women can overcome barriers and reach new levels of success in their careers.

ADVOCATING FOR YOURSELF AND OTHERS IN THE WORKPLACE

Advocating for yourself and others in the workplace is a crucial skill that everyone, regardless of gender, should possess. In the book "Breaking the Glass Ceiling: A Woman's Guide to Success," we delve into the importance of standing up for yourself and those around you in the professional world.

For women, advocating for yourself means speaking up when you deserve a raise or promotion, asserting your opinions in meetings, and not being afraid to take on challenging projects. It's about knowing your worth and not being afraid to demand what you deserve. By advocating for yourself, you not only advance your own career but also pave the way for other women in the workplace.

Men can also benefit from advocating for themselves and their female colleagues. By supporting gender equality initiatives, speaking out against discrimination, and actively promoting female coworkers, men can help create a more inclusive and diverse work environment. Advocating for gender equality benefits everyone in the workplace, not just women.

For parents, teaching your children the importance of advocating for themselves and others is crucial. By setting a positive example and encouraging your children to stand up for themselves and their beliefs, you are instilling valuable skills that will benefit them throughout their lives.

Teenagers, in particular, can benefit from learning how to advocate for themselves early on. By developing assertiveness and self-confidence, teenagers can navigate the challenges of school and eventually the workplace with ease.

In conclusion, advocating for yourself and others in the workplace is a powerful tool for empowerment and success. By standing up for what you believe in and supporting those around you, you can help break down barriers and create a more equitable and inclusive workplace for all.

CHAPTER 7: INSPIRING STORIES OF WOMEN IN LEADERSHIP

WOMEN IN CORPORATE LEADERSHIP

In the ever-evolving landscape of corporate leadership, women continue to break barriers and shatter glass ceilings. This subchapter focuses on the inspiring stories of women who have risen to the top of their respective fields, leading with confidence, resilience, and determination.

For women looking to advance in their careers, it is essential to have role models to look up to. The stories shared in this subchapter showcase the power of perseverance and the importance of believing in oneself. These women have proven that gender is not a barrier to success, and that with hard work and dedication, anything is possible.

Parents play a crucial role in shaping the future generation of female leaders. By instilling values of equality, ambition, and self-confidence in their daughters, parents can help pave the way for a more diverse and inclusive corporate landscape. Encouraging young girls to pursue their passions and dream big is key to fostering the next generation of women in leadership.

For teenagers, the stories shared in this subchapter serve as a source of inspiration and motivation. These women have faced challenges and overcome obstacles to reach the top of their fields, proving that anything is possible with perseverance and determination. By believing in themselves and their abilities, teenagers can set themselves on the path to success in the corporate world.

In the niche of feminism, the stories of women in corporate leadership highlight the ongoing fight for gender equality in the workplace. These women have defied stereotypes and pushed boundaries, paving the way for future generations of female leaders. Their stories serve as a reminder of the progress that has been made, as well as the work that still needs to be done to achieve true equality in the corporate world.

WOMEN IN ENTREPRENEURSHIP

Entrepreneurship has long been seen as a male-dominated field, but in recent years, women have been breaking through the glass ceiling and making their mark in the business world. In this subchapter, we will explore the challenges and triumphs of women in entrepreneurship, and how they are paving the way for future generations of female leaders.

One of the main challenges that women face in entrepreneurship is access to funding. Studies have shown that women entrepreneurs receive significantly less funding than their male counterparts, despite the fact that businesses founded by women often perform just as well, if not better, than those founded by men. This lack of funding can make it difficult for women to grow their businesses and reach their full potential.

However, despite these challenges, women in entrepreneurship have proven time and time again that they are more than capable of running successful businesses. From small startups to large corporations, women are making their mark in every industry imaginable. They are not only creating innovative products and services, but also prioritizing social responsibility and sustainability in their business practices.

For women, parents, and teenagers interested in pursuing a career in entrepreneurship, the stories of successful female entrepreneurs can be both inspiring and instructive. By learning from the experiences of these trailblazing women, aspiring entrepreneurs can gain valuable insights into what it takes to succeed in the business world.

In conclusion, women in entrepreneurship are breaking barriers, shattering stereotypes, and redefining what it means to be a leader in the business world. Their stories serve as a source of inspiration for women of all ages and backgrounds, and demonstrate the power of resilience, perseverance, and determination in achieving one's goals.

WOMEN IN POLITICS

Women have historically been underrepresented in the field of politics, facing numerous challenges and obstacles when trying to break into leadership roles. However, over the years, many inspiring women have shattered the glass ceiling and made their mark in the political arena. These trailblazers have paved the way for future generations of women to enter politics and make a difference in their communities.

One of the key factors that have held women back from pursuing political careers is the lack of representation and support. Gender biases and stereotypes have often deterred women from running for office or taking on leadership roles. However, it is crucial for women to be empowered and encouraged to participate in politics and have their voices heard.

CHAPTER 5: INSPIRING STORIES OF WOMEN IN LEADERSHIP

Women bring a unique perspective to the political landscape, advocating for issues that are often overlooked or marginalized. By having more women in politics, we can ensure that diverse voices are represented and that policies are reflective of the needs and concerns of all individuals in society.

For women, parents, and teenagers interested in getting involved in politics, it is important to seek out mentors and role models who have successfully navigated the political sphere. Networking with other women in politics and participating in leadership development programs can also help build the skills and confidence needed to succeed in this field.

By breaking the glass ceiling in politics, women can create a more inclusive and equitable society for all individuals. It is time for women to step up, take charge, and make a difference in the political arena. Together, we can build a better future for generations to come.

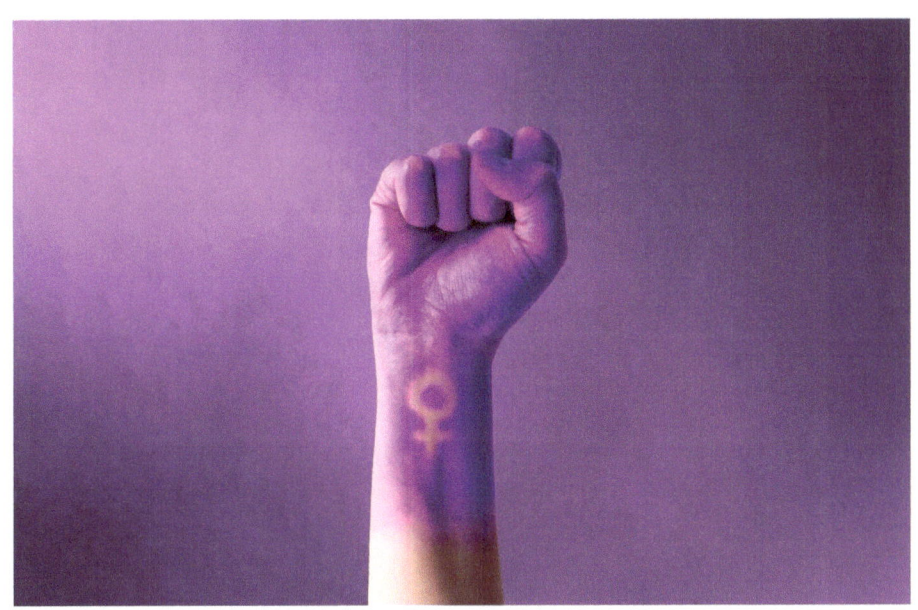

CHAPTER 8: EMPOWERING THE NEXT GENERATION

MENTORING AND SUPPORTING YOUNG WOMEN

Mentoring and supporting young women is a crucial aspect of breaking the glass ceiling and empowering future female leaders. As women who have successfully navigated the challenges of leadership, it is our responsibility to lift up the next generation and provide them with the tools and guidance they need to succeed.

In this subchapter, we will explore the various advantages that mentorship can provide for women in their career growth and personal empowerment.

CHAPTER 6: EMPOWERING THE NEXT GENERATION

Mentoring can take many forms, from one-on-one coaching sessions to group workshops and networking events. By sharing our own experiences, insights, and advice, we can help young women develop the skills and confidence they need to excel in their chosen fields. Whether it's negotiating a salary, speaking up in meetings, or balancing work and family commitments, we can offer guidance and support to help young women overcome obstacles and achieve their goals.

Supporting young women also means creating a culture that values and promotes their voices and contributions. By advocating for equal opportunities and representation in leadership positions, we can help create a more inclusive and diverse workplace for future generations. This includes challenging gender stereotypes, advocating for policies that support work-life balance, and fostering a culture of respect and support for all employees.

One of the key benefits of mentorship for women is access to guidance and support from experienced professionals who have navigated similar challenges in their own careers. Mentors can offer valuable insights, advice, and encouragement that can help women overcome obstacles and achieve their goals. By having a mentor, women can tap into a wealth of knowledge and expertise that can help them make informed decisions and avoid common pitfalls.

Additionally, mentorship can provide women with access to valuable networking opportunities and connections that can open doors to new career opportunities. Mentors can introduce women to key players in their industry, help them build relationships with potential collaborators or sponsors, and provide access to valuable resources and information that can help them succeed.

Furthermore, mentorship can also boost women's confidence and self-esteem, empowering them to take on new challenges and pursue their ambitions with greater determination and resilience. By having a mentor who believes in their potential and supports their growth, women can overcome self-doubt and imposter syndrome, and cultivate a strong sense of self-efficacy and self-worth.

As parents, it is important to instill in our daughters the belief that they are capable of achieving anything they set their minds to. By encouraging them to pursue their passions, take risks, and speak up for themselves, we can help them develop the confidence and resilience they need to succeed in a male-dominated world.

For teenagers, mentoring and support from older women can be invaluable in navigating the challenges of adolescence and preparing for the future. By connecting with female role models and seeking out opportunities for mentorship and guidance, young women can build the skills and relationships they need to succeed in school, work, and beyond.

In conclusion, mentoring and supporting young women is a powerful way to break the glass ceiling and create a more equitable and inclusive society for all. By sharing our knowledge, experiences, and resources with the next generation, we can help empower young women to reach their full potential and become the leaders of tomorrow.

BUILDING A STRONG PROFESSIONAL NETWORK

Building a strong professional network is essential for anyone looking to advance their career, but it can be particularly crucial for women striving to break through the glass ceiling. In a world where gender inequality still exists in many workplaces, having a solid support system of professional contacts can make all the difference in achieving success.

For women, in particular, networking can open up opportunities that may not be readily available through other channels. By connecting with like-minded individuals, mentors, and potential employers, women can gain valuable insights, advice, and even job leads that can help them advance in their careers.

To build a strong professional network, women (and men) should start by attending industry events, conferences, and networking mixers. These events provide a great opportunity to meet new people, exchange business cards, and make valuable connections. Additionally, joining professional organizations and online networking groups can also be a great way to expand your network and stay informed about industry trends.

Parents can also benefit from building a strong professional network, as it can provide them with a support system of other working parents who understand the challenges they face. By connecting with other parents in similar situations, they can share resources, advice, and even job opportunities that can help them balance work and family responsibilities.

For teenagers interested in pursuing a career in a male-dominated field, building a strong professional network early on can be instrumental in overcoming barriers and breaking through the glass ceiling. Encouraging young women to connect with mentors, teachers, and professionals in their desired field can help them gain valuable insights and support as they navigate their career paths.

In conclusion, building a strong professional network is essential for anyone looking to succeed in their career, but it can be particularly beneficial for women striving to break through the glass ceiling. By connecting with others in their field, women can gain valuable insights, support, and opportunities that can help them advance in their careers and achieve their goals.

CHAPTER 6: EMPOWERING THE NEXT GENERATION

FINDING AND BEING A MENTOR

Finding and being a mentor can be a game-changer in your journey to success. In the world of business and leadership, having a mentor can provide invaluable guidance, support, and opportunities for growth. As women, it is essential to seek out mentors who can help us navigate the unique challenges we face in male-dominated industries.

To find a mentor, start by identifying someone you admire and respect in your field. Reach out to them with a clear and concise request for mentorship, explaining why you believe they would be a great mentor for you. Be prepared to invest time and effort in building a relationship with your mentor, and be open to their guidance and feedback.

Being a mentor can also be a rewarding experience. As you climb the corporate ladder, remember to reach back and lift others up. By sharing your knowledge and experience with younger women, you can help them avoid pitfalls and achieve their goals more quickly.

For parents and teenagers, finding and being a mentor is equally important. Parents can serve as mentors to their children, providing guidance, support, and encouragement as they navigate their educational and career paths. Teenagers can seek out mentors in their desired fields, helping them to explore different career options and gain valuable insights into what it takes to succeed.

In the fight for gender equality, mentorship plays a critical role. By supporting and empowering one another, women can break through the glass ceiling and achieve their full potential. So, whether you are seeking a mentor or considering becoming one, remember that mentorship is a powerful tool for personal and professional growth.

CHAPTER 6: EMPOWERING THE NEXT GENERATION

EDUCATING GIRLS FOR LEADERSHIP

Empowering girls through education is a crucial step towards breaking the glass ceiling and achieving gender equality in leadership roles. The importance of educating girls for leadership cannot be overstated, as it lays the foundation for a more inclusive and diverse future.

When girls are given the tools and opportunities to excel academically, they are better equipped to take on leadership roles in various sectors. By investing in girls' education, we are investing in the future leaders who will drive positive change in our society.

For women, parents, and teenagers, it is essential to recognize the value of education in shaping future leaders. Encouraging girls to pursue their passions and excel in their studies is a powerful way to instill confidence and leadership skills from a young age.

Feminism plays a crucial role in advocating for equal access to education for girls. By dismantling societal barriers and challenging stereotypes, feminists can create a more inclusive and supportive environment for girls to thrive academically and professionally.

In "Breaking the Glass Ceiling: A Woman's Guide to Success," we highlight the stories of women who have overcome obstacles and shattered stereotypes to become leaders in their fields. These stories serve as inspiration for girls, parents, and teenagers, showing them that anything is possible with determination and hard work.

By educating girls for leadership, we are not only empowering individuals but also creating a more just and equitable society for all. Let us continue to support and uplift the next generation of female leaders, ensuring that they have the tools and opportunities to reach their full potential.

FOSTERING AN INCLUSIVE WORK ENVIRONMENT

Fostering an inclusive work environment is crucial for breaking down barriers and promoting equality in the workplace. In this subchapter, we will explore the importance of creating a culture that values diversity and empowers women to excel in leadership roles.

To truly foster an inclusive work environment, it is essential to recognize and address unconscious biases that may exist within the organization. By promoting awareness and education around these biases, we can create a more equitable workplace where all employees feel valued and respected.

One way to promote inclusivity is through mentorship and sponsorship programs that support women in their career development. By providing opportunities for networking and professional growth, organizations can help women break through the glass ceiling and reach their full potential.

Additionally, creating a supportive work culture that values work–life balance is essential for fostering inclusivity. By offering flexible work arrangements and family–friendly policies, organizations can empower women to succeed both professionally and personally.

As women, parents, and teenagers, it is important to advocate for inclusivity in the workplace and support initiatives that promote gender equality. By working together to challenge stereotypes and promote diversity, we can create a more inclusive and equitable work environment for all.

In conclusion, fostering an inclusive work environment is essential for breaking the glass ceiling and empowering women to thrive in leadership roles. By promoting awareness, providing support, and advocating for change, we can create a more inclusive and equitable workplace for future generations.

CHAPTER 9: BREAKING THE GLASS CEILING TOGETHER

ADVOCATING FOR GENDER EQUALITY

In today's society, the fight for gender equality is more important than ever. Women have made great strides in breaking the glass ceiling and shattering stereotypes, but there is still much work to be done. Advocating for gender equality is not just a matter of fairness, but a necessity for creating a more inclusive and progressive world for future generations.

Women, men, parents, and teenagers all have a role to play in advocating for gender equality. For women, it is important to continue to push boundaries and challenge societal norms. By speaking up, demanding equal pay, and taking on leadership roles, women can inspire others to do the same. Parents play a crucial role in teaching their children about respect, equality, and diversity. By raising children who understand the importance of gender equality, parents can help create a more inclusive and accepting society.

Teenagers, in particular, have the power to shape the future of gender equality. By educating themselves on feminist issues, speaking out against discrimination, and supporting women in leadership roles, teenagers can make a real difference in the fight for gender equality. Empowering young women to pursue their dreams and break down barriers is essential for creating a more equal future.

Feminism is not just a buzzword — it is a movement that seeks to dismantle oppressive systems and create a more just and equitable society for all. By advocating for gender equality, women, parents, and teenagers can help pave the way for a brighter future where everyone has the opportunity to succeed, regardless of their gender. Let us continue to break down barriers and inspire the next generation of leaders to rise up and make a difference.

PROGRESS MADE IN GENDER EQUALITY

In recent years, there have been significant strides made in the fight for gender equality. Women all around the world are breaking barriers, shattering stereotypes, and making their voices heard in ways that were once unimaginable. This progress is not only empowering for women but also beneficial for society as a whole.

One of the most notable achievements in gender equality is the increase in women's representation in leadership positions. Women are now serving as CEOs, politicians, scientists, and other traditionally male-dominated roles. This not only showcases the capabilities of women but also provides role models for the younger generation to aspire to.

Additionally, there has been a shift in societal attitudes towards gender roles and expectations. Men are now more involved in caregiving and household responsibilities, while women are encouraged to pursue their career goals without fear of judgment or discrimination. This shift has created a more equal playing field for both men and women to thrive in all aspects of life.

Parents play a crucial role in shaping the future of gender equality by teaching their children about respect, empathy, and the importance of equal opportunities. By instilling these values in their children from a young age, parents can help create a more inclusive and equitable society for future generations.

For teenagers, this progress in gender equality offers hope and inspiration for a brighter future. They can see that their gender should not limit their aspirations or potential, and that they have the power to create positive change in the world.

Overall, the progress made in gender equality is a testament to the resilience and determination of women everywhere. By continuing to push for equality and support one another, we can create a more just and equitable world for all.

COLLABORATING WITH MALE ALLIES

In the fight for gender equality, collaboration with male allies is crucial. "Breaking the Glass Ceiling: A Woman's Guide to Success" emphasizes the importance of working together with men to create a more inclusive and equitable society.

For women, having male allies can provide valuable support and amplify their voices in male-dominated spaces. By forming alliances with men who share their values and beliefs, women can challenge the status quo and break down barriers that prevent them from reaching their full potential. Male allies can use their privilege to advocate for gender equality, challenge harmful stereotypes, and create opportunities for women to advance in their careers.

CHAPTER 7: BREAKING THE GLASS CEILING TOGETHER

Parents play a crucial role in teaching their children about the importance of gender equality and collaborating with male allies. By modeling respectful and equal partnerships at home, parents can instill values of respect, empathy, and inclusivity in their children. Encouraging teenagers to engage in conversations about feminism and allyship can help them develop a deeper understanding of the issues facing women and the importance of working together to create a more just society.

For those interested in feminism, collaborating with male allies can help amplify their message and create a more inclusive movement. By working together, women and men can challenge harmful stereotypes, dismantle systemic barriers, and create a more equitable world for all genders.

In "Breaking the Glass Ceiling: A Woman's Guide to Success," readers are encouraged to seek out male allies who are committed to gender equality and collaborate with them to create positive change. By working together, we can break down the barriers that hold women back and create a more inclusive and equitable society for all.

SUSTAINING PROGRESS IN WOMEN'S LEADERSHIP

In a world where women are still underrepresented in leadership positions, it is crucial to sustain the progress that has been made in breaking the glass ceiling. As we continue to strive for gender equality, it is important for women to support and uplift each other in their journey towards leadership roles.

One of the key ways to sustain progress in women's leadership is by mentoring and empowering the next generation of female leaders. By sharing our experiences and offering guidance to young women, we can help them navigate the challenges they may face in their careers. As women, we must also continue to advocate for policies and initiatives that promote gender equality in the workplace.

CHAPTER 7: BREAKING THE GLASS CEILING TOGETHER

Parents play a crucial role in shaping the future of women's leadership. By instilling values of equality and resilience in their children, parents can help cultivate a generation of strong and confident women leaders. It is important for parents to encourage their daughters to dream big and pursue their ambitions, regardless of any societal barriers they may face.

For teenagers, it is essential to recognize the importance of women's leadership and the impact it can have on society as a whole. By learning about the achievements of women leaders and understanding the challenges they have overcome, teenagers can be inspired to follow in their footsteps and strive for their own success.

In the realm of feminism, sustaining progress in women's leadership means continuing to push for equality and representation in all aspects of society. By working together and supporting one another, women can break down barriers and shatter stereotypes that have held them back for far too long.

As we look towards the future, let us remember the importance of sustaining progress in women's leadership. By empowering the next generation, advocating for gender equality, and supporting one another, we can continue to break the glass ceiling and inspire change for generations to come.

LEADERSHIP QUALITIES FOR WOMEN

Leadership qualities for women are essential in breaking the glass ceiling and achieving success in male-dominated industries. In this subchapter, we will explore the key traits and characteristics that women should cultivate to become effective leaders in their careers.

One of the most important leadership qualities for women is confidence. Women must believe in themselves and their abilities in order to inspire and motivate others. Confidence is contagious, and when women exude self-assurance, they are more likely to earn the respect and trust of their colleagues and superiors.

Another crucial leadership quality for women is resilience. In the face of adversity and challenges, women must be able to bounce back and persevere. Resilient leaders are able to weather the storms and stay focused on their goals, even when the going gets tough.

Empathy and emotional intelligence are also key leadership qualities for women. Women are often more in tune with the emotions and needs of others, making them adept at building strong relationships and fostering collaboration. By being empathetic and emotionally intelligent, women can create inclusive and supportive work environments where everyone can thrive.

Effective communication skills are essential for women leaders to convey their vision, goals, and expectations clearly to their teams. Women must be able to articulate their ideas and thoughts with confidence and clarity, inspiring others to follow their lead.

Lastly, women leaders must be adaptable and open to change. In today's fast-paced and ever-changing business world, the ability to pivot and innovate is crucial for success. By embracing change and being open to new ideas and ways of working, women can stay ahead of the curve and lead their teams to success.

Overall, by cultivating these leadership qualities, women can break the glass ceiling, shatter stereotypes, and pave the way for a more inclusive and equal future.

INSPIRING AND EMPOWERING YOUR COLLEAGUES

In the corporate world, inspiring and empowering your colleagues is not only a sign of strong leadership, but also a key factor in creating a positive and productive work environment. As women

CHAPTER 7: BREAKING THE GLASS CEILING TOGETHER

navigating the often male-dominated workplace, it is important to lift each other up and support one another in our professional journeys. By empowering our colleagues, we can break down barriers and shatter the glass ceiling that has long held us back.

For women, inspiring and empowering our colleagues means advocating for gender equality and promoting diversity in the workplace. It means standing up for ourselves and for each other in the face of discrimination or bias. By supporting and uplifting our fellow female colleagues, we can create a more inclusive and equitable work environment where everyone has the opportunity to succeed.

For men, inspiring and empowering your female colleagues means being an ally and champion for gender equality. It means listening to their voices and experiences, and using your privilege to create space for them to thrive. By actively supporting and advocating for your female colleagues, you can help to create a more diverse and inclusive workplace where everyone feels valued and respected.

For parents and teenagers, inspiring and empowering your colleagues means leading by example and showing them the importance of supporting one another. By teaching the next generation the value of teamwork and collaboration, we can create a more inclusive and equitable future for all. By instilling these values in our children, we can help to break down barriers and create a more equal society for future generations to come.

In conclusion, inspiring and empowering your colleagues is not only a powerful act of leadership, but also a necessary step towards creating a more inclusive and equitable workplace. By supporting and lifting each other up, we can break through the glass ceiling and pave the way for a more equal future for all.

CHAPTER 10: CONCLUSION

REFLECTIONS ON BREAKING THE GLASS CEILING

In this subchapter, we delve into the powerful and inspiring stories of women who have shattered the glass ceiling in their respective fields. These women have defied societal expectations and limitations to rise to the top of their professions, paving the way for future generations of women to do the same.

For women, this subchapter serves as a reminder that no dream is too big, and no obstacle is too insurmountable. The stories shared here are a testament to the strength, resilience, and determination of women who refuse to be held back by gender stereotypes or biases. They serve as beacons of hope and inspiration for women everywhere, showing that it is possible to achieve success and leadership roles in male-dominated industries.

CHAPTER 8: CONCLUSION

For parents, this subchapter offers valuable insights into the importance of supporting and empowering their daughters to pursue their ambitions and break through barriers. By encouraging young girls to dream big and reach for the stars, parents can help cultivate the next generation of female leaders who will continue to push boundaries and challenge the status quo.

For teenagers, this subchapter provides a glimpse into the possibilities that lie ahead and the potential for greatness that resides within each of them. It shows them that they have the power to shape their own destinies and make a difference in the world, no matter what challenges they may face.

In the niche of feminism, this subchapter underscores the ongoing struggle for gender equality and the importance of dismantling the barriers that prevent women from reaching their full potential. It calls on feminists to continue fighting for equal rights and opportunities for women in all aspects of society, so that one day the glass ceiling will be nothing more than a distant memory.

MOVING FORWARD WITH CONFIDENCE AND DETERMINATION

The subchapter "Moving Forward with Confidence and Determination" is a powerful reminder to women, parents, and teenagers that they have the strength and resilience to break through any barriers that stand in their way. In a world where gender equality is still an ongoing battle, it is crucial for women to embrace their capabilities and push forward with unwavering determination.

For women who aspire to leadership positions, it is important to cultivate a sense of confidence in their abilities. They must believe in themselves and their worth, despite any doubts or obstacles that may come their way. By moving forward with confidence, women can inspire others and pave the way for future generations of female leaders.

CHAPTER 8: CONCLUSION

Parents play a crucial role in nurturing their daughters' self-esteem and confidence. By encouraging them to pursue their passions and dreams, parents can empower their daughters to believe in themselves and strive for success. It is important for parents to instill in their children the belief that they are capable of achieving anything they set their minds to.

For teenagers, the subchapter serves as a reminder that they have the power to shape their futures and break through the glass ceiling. By cultivating a sense of determination and perseverance, teenagers can overcome any challenges that come their way and achieve their goals. It is important for teenagers to believe in themselves and their abilities, even when faced with adversity.

In the realm of feminism, the subchapter highlights the importance of women supporting and uplifting each other. By coming together and standing united, women can break down barriers and create a more inclusive and equitable society. By moving forward with confidence and determination, women can continue to shatter the glass ceiling and inspire change for generations to come.

CHALLENGES AND BARRIERS THAT STILL EXIST

Despite the progress that has been made in the fight for gender equality, there are still many challenges and barriers that women face in their quest for success. In this subchapter, we will explore some of the key obstacles that still exist and offer strategies for overcoming them.

One of the biggest challenges that women face is the pervasive gender bias that continues to exist in many workplaces. Women are often judged more harshly than men and are held to higher standards. This can make it difficult for women to advance in their careers and can lead to feelings of imposter syndrome.

Another barrier that women face is the lack of representation in leadership roles. Despite making up nearly half of the workforce, women are significantly underrepresented in senior management positions. This lack of representation can make it difficult for women to find mentors and sponsors who can help them advance in their careers.

Additionally, the gender pay gap continues to be a significant issue for women. On average, women earn just 82 cents for every dollar earned by men. This disparity not only affects women's financial security but also their ability to advance in their careers.

For parents, balancing work and family responsibilities can be a major challenge. Women are often expected to juggle their careers with caregiving responsibilities, which can make it difficult to advance in their careers. This can be especially challenging for single parents or those without access to affordable childcare.

For teenagers, societal expectations and stereotypes can create barriers to success. Many young girls are still socialized to believe that certain careers are off-limits to them, leading to a lack of confidence and ambition. It is important to challenge these stereotypes and encourage young women to pursue their passions and dreams.

In order to break through these barriers, women must continue to advocate for themselves and support one another. By working together and challenging the status quo, we can create a more equitable and inclusive world for future generations.

STEPS TO CONTINUE BREAKING THE GLASS CEILING

In order to continue breaking the glass ceiling and shatter the barriers that have held women back in the workplace, there are several key steps that individuals can take to drive change and promote gender equality. Here are some important strategies to consider:

1. Advocate for Yourself: It's important to speak up for yourself and make your accomplishments known. Don't be afraid to ask for promotions, raises, or opportunities for advancement. By advocating for yourself, you can show your value and potential to your superiors.

2. Support Other Women: In addition to advocating for yourself, it's crucial to support other women in the workplace. This can involve mentoring, networking, or simply being a supportive colleague. By lifting each other up, women can create a stronger, more inclusive work environment.

3. Challenge Stereotypes: It's important to challenge stereotypes and biases that may exist in the workplace. This can involve speaking out against discriminatory practices, promoting diversity and inclusion, and educating others about the importance of gender equality.

4. Seek Out Leadership Opportunities: Women should actively seek out leadership opportunities and positions of power within their organizations. By taking on leadership roles, women can help shape the culture of their workplace and promote gender equality from the top down.

5. Encourage the Next Generation: Parents and teenagers can play a crucial role in breaking the glass ceiling by encouraging young women to pursue their goals and dreams. By instilling confidence and ambition in the next generation, we can create a more equal and inclusive society for all.

By following these steps and working together to promote gender equality, we can continue to break the glass ceiling and create a more equitable world for women everywhere.